SEVEN PILLARS
FOR SUCCESSFUL
SERVICE

WILLIAM E. THRASHER, JR.

WESTBOW
PRESS®
A DIVISION OF THOMAS NELSON
& ZONDERVAN

WestBow Press books may be ordered through booksellers or by contacting:

WestBow Press
A Division of Thomas Nelson & Zondervan
1663 Liberty Drive
Bloomington, IN 47403
www.westbowpress.com
844-714-3454

Scripture taken from the King James Version of the Bible.

ISBN: 978-1-6642-1569-6 (sc)
ISBN: 978-1-6642-1570-2 (e)

Library of Congress Control Number: 2020924421

Print information available on the last page.

WestBow Press rev. date: 1/4/2021

This book is dedicated to First Baptist Church 901 Calhoun Street in Little Rock, Arkansas, without whom this book would not be possible.

Wisdom hath builded her house, she
hath hewn out her seven pillars.
—Proverbs 9:1

CONTENTS

FOREWORD

What an easy read with practical suggestions for the young pastor is found in **Seven Pillars For Successful Service.** Time is always of the essence whether one is beginning ministry or exploring restructuring. To have the first hand experience of a first time pastor who was born in the church, but who has experienced the world is very much a plus. My conscious memory can't recall a moment that I haven't known the Rev. William Edward Thrasher, Jr, my brother from another mother, my lifelong friend and colleague in ministry. I am honored and humbled to have been invited to write this foreword. I admire his courage and commitment to present this book as a means of paying it forward to those entering ministry. I pray that this book will be as helpful to you as the process that William has undergone to produce it. I believe in William; I trust William, In this age of longings and yearnings, here is a book written on a solid and firm foundation secured with truth. I pray it will give you insights for ministry as you discern who God is calling you to be in the place where God has placed you to shepherd His people.

Ralph E. Blanks, Pastor
Vine Memorial Baptist Church
Philadelphia, PA

PREFACE

Seven Pillars for Successful Service was not written to be an exercise in scholarship but a simple handbook designed to help first-time pastors and developing churches focus on the fundamental ingredients that define the character of any church. Since no two churches are the same, it follows that the needs for each church will not be the same. This handbook should be an excellent aid in helping to identify strengths and weaknesses of a particular church and provide guidance while building on the strengths and strengthening the weaknesses.

Though this book is scripturally based, you are encouraged to research each pillar personally and draw from it God's specific message for you. I trust that in your perusal of *Seven Pillars for Successful Service*, you will find God's lamp for your feet and His light for your path and that these few printed words will be a source of hope and enlightenment.

MINISTRY OBJECTIVES AND STRATEGIES

Go ye therefore, and teach all nations, baptizing

them in the name of the Father and of the Son and

the Holy Ghost: Teaching them to observe all things

whatsoever I have commanded you: and lo, I am

with you alway, even unto the end of the world.

—Matthew 28:19-20

The ultimate objective of the Christian church is to carry out the "Great Commission" as commanded by Christ. Paul, commenting on how that objective is to be realized, said, "We are to become all things to all men that we might by all means save some." The purpose of this book is to provide a focus for first-time pastors or developing churches who are striving to reach the ultimate objective but who also may become overwhelmed by what appears to be a daunting task.

Seven Pillars for Successful Service is a what and why book more than a how-to book. However, it is designed so that you can make comparative notes between the written material and what exists within your present church structure. I believe that the information provided here, if taken to heart, will help eliminate the frustration often experienced by young pastors and developing churches in the pursuit of their mission.

Seven key elements, which I refer to as *pillars,* undergird the basic structure of the church. Defined as a support base, a source of stability, or a foundation, the term *pillar,* as used in this text, means strength. Clearly, all three definitions are applicable to this text. The seven pillars provide support, stability, and a firm foundation, which will lead to *successful service* for your church. These seven pillars are church administration, Christian education, parishioner welfare, stewardship, temple maintenance, Christian fellowship, and the ministry of worship. It takes all seven pillars working in concert to achieve successful service in order to win souls for Christ.

Keeping the primary objective in mind, that of bringing people to Christ, we will look at each of the seven pillars for successful service to understand their role in reaching the ultimate objective.

PILLAR 1

Church Administration

Brethren, be followers together of me, and
mark them which walk so as ye have us
for an example.
—Philippians 3:17

This first pillar is comprised of the pastor, deacons, and heads of auxiliaries. The deacons and ministry leaders are the primary support base of the pastor. The goal for this group is to work harmoniously together, providing the kind of Christian leadership that church people will want to follow. The leadership of the church should meet monthly for planning the upcoming month's activities, minimizing possible conflicts. I recommend that church meetings with the body convene quarterly.

In the interim, monthly newsletters, emails, or whatever electronic communication is your preference should be used, followed up by direct contact by assigned deacons.

It will be the responsibility of the leadership (pastors, deacons, and ministry leaders) to set up the calendar on an annual basis and select ministry participants to head each of the major annual observances. All ministry leaders should be actively engaged in the church's Christian education ministry. They should be strong supporters of the prayer life of the church, and they should all be tithers.

While no two churches are identical, there are basic similarities, which are represented by the following examples of church organizational structures:

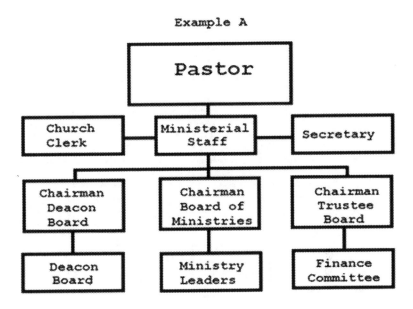

Example A

Pastor

Church Clerk — Ministerial Staff — Secretary

Chairman Deacon Board | Chairman Board of Ministries | Chairman Trustee Board

Deacon Board | Ministry Leaders | Finance Committee

You will note that under example A are three officers who report directly to the pastor. They are the chairmen of the deacon board, board of ministries, and trustees. In my opinion, this is the ideal organizational structure because it allows for equal access as well as attention to the pastor by those leaders directly responsible for coordinating the activities of the various ministries that maintain the integrity of the seven pillars.

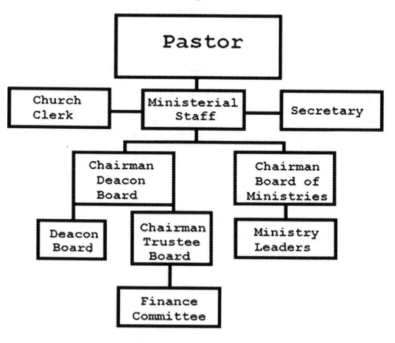

Organizational chart B represents the more traditional church structure. This approach works well for the pastor who likes a more streamlined administration. Please be reminded that these are just two examples out of many. The important thing to remember is that you find what works best for your particular situation.

As the above scripture suggests, we leaders are to be examples that command the kind of respect worthy of following. Leadership means to *lead* the way rather than follow the way. Regardless of the undertaking, the pastor and the deacons should be at the frontline not only showing support, but also putting into usable action the urgency for success of the tasks at hand.

NOTES

PILLAR 2

Christian Education

Study to shew thyself approved unto God, a
workman that needeth not to be ashamed,
rightly dividing the word of truth.
—2 Timothy 2:15

Christian education is the source of light for the church.
Our personal lights will not shine without it. The Great
Commission cannot be realized without it, and God's
stamp of approval demands it. It is through the study of
the Word that we are better able to share God's divine
design for human salvation. It is through Christian
education that our witnessing efforts will succeed. The
Christian education ministry is headed by the pastor
and the board of Christian education. The makeup of

the BCE (board of Christian education) consists of those members who are directly involved in the education of the church body. This includes the superintendent of the Sunday school, the Sunday school staff, and other volunteers who are committed to rightly dividing the word of truth.

The BCE is also responsible for providing educational support to the various ministries within the church. This entails locating the proper training materials and coordination of workshops for implementation of the training. As was previously stated, it is through Christian education that our witnessing efforts will succeed. For this to occur, the BCE, with the guidance of the pastor, should develop the church's evangelistic/outreach ministry. This responsibility involves the preparation of witnessing teams, providing strategic planning, and appropriate training materials that will inspire the teams as well as increase their effectiveness.

Developing an aggressive bus ministry also falls within this area of responsibility. The BCE should be responsible for undergirding the youth department of the church, which should include, but not be limited to, the development of a singles ministry, couples ministry, youth outreach ministry, and tutorial program for students within the church community. The BCE is also responsible for seeing that the youth department participates in district, state, and national association work, if the church is so affiliated.

Additionally, the BCE will provide assistance to developing ministries within the church, such as the school adoption ministry, for tracking youth challenged with social and behavioral issues, and the community athletics ministry.

As you can see, the BCE plays a vital role in the life of the church internally and the church's relationship with the greater community as well.

Finally, it is the responsibility of the BCE to set up and staff the church's library and appoint a church historian. Obviously, the purpose of the library is to provide the proper tools to enhance the facilitation of Christian education within the church.

The church historian's responsibility is to put down

in writing in as much detail as is possible regarding how the church was started and how it has progressed. An appreciation of the church's history can only help provide a better focus on the church's future.

The BCE should provide to the pastor its goals and timetables indicating the implementation of its objectives for each year. Also included in this report should be a realistic budget reflecting the projected cost to finance their ministries.

NOTES

PILLAR 3

Parishioner Welfare

Pure religion and undefiled before God
and the Father is this, To visit the fatherless
and widows in their affliction, and to keep
himself unspotted from the world.

—James 1:27

Parishioner welfare, it could be said, was born in the spirit of the Word. It is pure religion in action. Jesus taught that as often as we feed the hungry, clothe the naked, and visit the sick and imprisoned, we are doing these things unto him. This *pillar* is a vital link in building a great chain for Christ and is the overall scheme of *successful service*. Several ministries overlap in the fulfilling of this work. The primary weight, however, is placed on the deacon board. Through the deacons ministry, the welfare of every member of the church and community can be attended to. Each deacon should be assigned a certain number of parishioners to keep the pastor abreast of every member of the church, and likewise, keep the church body informed of the condition of its fellow members. In addition to the deacon board, the mission society ministry, the junior women's mission, and young men's ministry should also share in the responsibility to visit the sick and shut-in and to offer whatever assistance they can provide. During this current pandemic, it is understandable that personal visitations must be curtailed for health and safety measures.

Perhaps the greatest statement that the church can make to its members and to the community in which it serves is how well it cares for its neighbors.

This type of involvement by the church communicates that there is real substance to what you believe and it instills confidence in both the membership and the community. In fact, when a church has a committed parishioner welfare ministry in place, it is planting seeds for *successful service.*

NOTES

PILLAR 4

Stewardship

Thus speak unto the Levites, and say unto them,
When ye take of the children of Israel the tithes
which I have given you from them for your
inheritance, then ye shall offer up an heave offering
of it for the Lord, even a tenth part of the tithe.
—Numbers 18:26

The ecclesiastic once said, "A feast is made for laughter, and wine maketh merry: but money answereth all things" (Ecclesiastes 10:19). Not only is this true in our personal lives, but it is equally true in the life of the church. The scriptures teach us that the church should be supported by tithes and offerings. In Malachi 3:10, the Lord says, "Bring ye all the tithes into the storage house that there may be meat in mine house ..." This scripture ensures that there is enough financial support to take care of the needs of the church. While the members of the finance committee are designated stewards responsible for administration of the church's monetary resources, it is the duty of every Christian to be obedient in this aspect of service as in every other aspect of the Christian experience.

The scripture not only directs the individual to tithe but instructs the church to tithe as well. Based on Numbers 18:26, I suggest that 10 percent of the church weekly income be set aside for the purpose of supporting the church's various missions (benevolent, home, district, state, national, and foreign). This represents "a tenth part of the tithe." This 10 percent should be distributed equally among the various ministries. If your church supports a national convention, the church tithe will at least give you some idea of how you can regularly support the ongoing work of the various ministries nationally and worldwide. By participating in this program on a monthly basis, you will find that this will simplify

William E. Thrasher, Jr.

your budgeting process and simplify the short-term and long-range commitments requested for support of your national work.

To ensure that the finance committee has at its disposal every available alternative for good money management, the church should consult a certified public accountant to review your present status and to make recommendations on how best to take full advantage your financial resources.

NOTES

PILLAR 5

Temple Maintenance

How amiable are thy tabernacles. O Lord of host!

—Psalm 84:1

The psalmist describes the Lord's house as being lovely. Since it is the Lord's house, it should be maintained in that manner. The care we take in the upkeep of the temple is a reflection of our affection and love for God. Take pride in the blessing the Lord has bestowed upon you, and let your appreciation show in how well you maintain the building and grounds.

In addition to your normal maintenance program, a church beautification ministry, comprised of members who have an eye for decorating, come together to add those special touches as the need arises. One suggestion on how to get support for this ministry would be to have members come together in the month of their birth to become the support staff during the month. It is not too far-fetched to assume that this could very likely entail volunteers staying a few minutes after each service to gather up left-behind programs or other discarded materials from the pews and the church grounds.

Temple maintenance not only involves physical care but behavior as well. Since each church has its own rules regarding behavior, just the mention of it is enough said.

NOTES

PILLAR 6

Christian Fellowship

Behold, how good and how pleasant it is
for brethren to dwell together in unity!
—Psalm 133:1

Christian fellowship promotes unity. The more we fellowship together, the stronger our bond of unity becomes. To foster more opportunities for Christian fellowship, in addition to the special occasions already designated on the church calendar, I suggest regular time be set aside to focus on the families via a family fellowship service. These services would address family dynamics aimed at building stronger Christ-centered families. Additionally, such activities as potluck dinners and picnics would also help foster meaningful fellowship.

25

The family fellowship ministry should consult the board of Christian education to assist in developing materials that would encourage consistent participation by the church body.

In recent years, many mainline Protestant churches have experienced a decline in both membership and appeal. To combat this decline and to stimulate growth, today's church must become more aggressive in its approach to provide Christian fellowship. The church must be willing to extend its arms of fellowship beyond its four walls. By showing the community your church's commitment to inclusiveness, you engender their hearts to your cause, thus furthering the church's understanding of the vital role that Christian fellowship plays in the life and times of the church.

With that being said, imagine the positive impact this will have on your ministry of evangelism, which is the ultimate objective of successful service.

NOTES

Ministry of Worship

God is a Spirit: and they that worship Him
must worship Him in spirit and in truth.
—John 4:24

Finally, we come to the ministry of worship. Pillar 7 is the result of all its predecessors.

Leadership has a strong impact on worship experience. When the congregation witnesses the church leaders fully engaged in the worship service from the morning praise to the benediction, that sends the message of just how powerful the role of worship is in the successful service of the whole ministry. *Christian education* prepares their hearts and their minds. It nourishes their spiritual health. Remember the scripture teaches, "My people are destroyed from a lack of knowledge" (Hosea 4:6).

The Word of God is fortifying, and spiritually fortified worshippers make for a dynamic, Spirit-filled worship experience. Good and faithful *stewardship* ensures that the provisions necessary for worship (comfortable environment, adequate audio and visual equipment functioning properly, etc.) are indeed in place to enhance the overall worship experience.

Temple maintenance plays a vital role in the atmosphere for successful worship. A pristine appearance of the sanctuary will ensure that unnecessary distractions won't take away from the worship service.

Christian fellowship bonds the body of Christ together in Christian love as one family. And when the family is together on one accord, that invites the presence of the Holy Spirit to be in the worship experience. To further the goad of a Spirit-filled worship experience, I recommend that everyone involved in the worship ministry (the choirs, the ushers, and the leadership) be active participants in Christian education. In order to worship the Lord in spirit and truth, we must be able to rightly divide the word, and that is not possible without studying to show yourself approved. In other words, you have got to know the Word!

During worship service, the ushers, even while the pastor is preaching, must keep watchful eyes on the needs of the congregation. If mothers with infants need assistance, the ushers are to make every effort to be at their disposal. If you have soundproof facilities within your sanctuary, use them. The congregation should also be mindful of the disruption excessive walking creates during the worship service.

Your Sunday morning worship can and will be a truly Spirit-filled experience if it is preceded by a strong praise service as well as a strong prayer life within the body. There can never be too much emphasis placed on the critical role that prayer has in maintaining a solid spiritual foundation. And when all of the seven pillars for successful service are working in harmony, the ultimate objective of reaching teaching and saving will be realized.

NOTES

AUTHOR BIO

William E. Thrasher Jr. was born in Little Rock, Arkansas. He is the second of seven children born to the late William E. Thrasher Sr. and the late Willie Mae Thrasher Hearon. He is a graduate of the University of Arkansas at Little Rock, is former pastor of First Baptist Church at 901 Calhoun Street in Little Rock, and currently resides in San

Antonio, Texas. He is the author of *To Make the Moment Last: The Story of the Incredible Jades*, *Good Citizenship for Today: A Mind Set on Civil Virtue*, *I Am Determined*, and now *Seven Pillars for Successful Service*. This current work was born out of his own experience as a first-time pastor charged with the challenging task of understanding what steps should be taken to give him a sense of direction.

Printed in the United States
By Bookmasters